SMART WORDS
READER

WEATHER AND CLIMATE

Christine A. Caputo

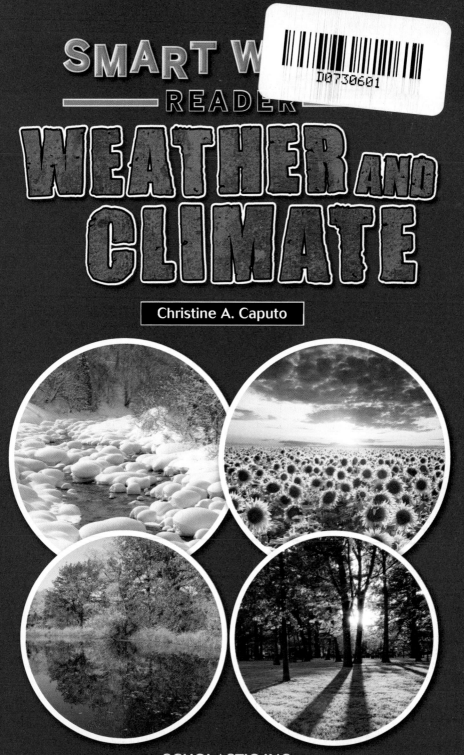

SCHOLASTIC INC.
New York Toronto London Auckland
Sydney Mexico City New Delhi Hong Kong

What are SMART WORDS?

Smart Words are frequently used words that are critical to understanding concepts taught in the classroom. The more Smart Words a child knows, the more easily he or she will grasp important curriculum concepts. Smart Words Readers introduce these key words in a fun and motivational format while developing important literacy skills. Each new word is highlighted, defined in context, and reviewed. Engaging activities at the end of each chapter allow readers to practice the words they have learned.

ISBN   978-0-545-36815-5

Packaged by Q2AMedia

Copyright © 2011 by Scholastic Inc.

Picture Credit: t= top, b= bottom, l= left, r= right, c= center

Cover Page: Frank van den Bergh/Istockphoto.
Title Page: Hidetoishyama/Fotolia; Haar Ctpyk/Istockphoto; Stta/Fotolia; Elena Elisseeva/Shutterstock.
Content Page: Liudmila Gridina /Shutterstock.

4t: Shutterstock; 4b: Lenice Harms/Shutterstock; 5: Lucian Coman/Shutterstock; 8-9: Sydney James/Digital Vision/Thinkstock; 10: Pklimenko/Dreamstime; 11: Colin D Young Lighting & Photography/stockphoto; 12l: Shutterstock; 12r: Lucian Coman/Shutterstock; 13: NASA; Ifong/Shutterstock; NASA; Maria Dryfhout /Shutterstock; Snaprender/Shutterstock; 14: Gertje Kappert/Fotolia; 16l: Robyn Waserman/National Science Foundation/USAP; 16r: John R Smith/Shutterstock; 17: Manamana / Shutterstock; 18t: Istockphoto/Thinkstock; 19t: Paulo Cruz/Shutterstock; 19b: Durdenimages/Dreamstime; 18-19: Helmut Konrad Watson/Shutterstock; 20: Istockphoto/Thinkstock; 21t: Volodymyr Goinyk/Shutterstock; 21c: Pavol Kmeto/Dreamstime; 21b: Kushnirov Avraham/Dreamstime; 22: NASA; 23t: JW.Alker / Photolibrary; 23b: D. Ducros/European Space Agency; 24: Petr Masek/Shutterstock; 26: Ng Han Guan/Associated Press/AP Images; 27: Sukree Sukplang/Reuters; 28: Olga Lipatova/Shutterstock; 29t: Pedrosala/Fotolia; 29c: BanksPhotos/Istockphoto; 29b: Nomadimages/Dreamstime; 30-31: Mike Norton/Shutterstock.

Q2AMedia Art Bank: 4-5, 6, 7, 8, 10, 15, 25.

12 11 10 9 8 7 6 5 4 3 2 1   11 12 13 14 15 16/0

Printed in the U.S.A.   40
First printing, September 2011

Table of Contents

Chapter 1

How's the Weather?

What should you wear today? Do you need a heavy coat or only a light shirt? Should you bring an umbrella or do you need your sunglasses? The answers to these questions depend on the conditions of the air outside.

North America

South America

Earth is surrounded by a blanket of air called the **atmosphere**. The condition of the atmosphere at any given time is known as **weather**. *Warm, cold, windy,* and *rainy* are words you might use to describe the weather.

Weather can change within a day, or even a few hours. However, the **climate** in a region describes the average weather conditions over a long period of time. Scientists usually use a 30-year time period to measure climate.

The climate in one region might be cold for most of the year. In another, it might be warm all the time. Climate affects what types of plants and animals are found in a region.

Europe

Asia

Africa

Australia

tarctica

SMART WORDS

atmosphere   the blanket of air that surrounds Earth

weather   the condition of the atmosphere at any given time in a particular location

climate   the long-term weather conditions in a region

What Causes the Weather?

The sun not only keeps Earth comfortable; it also drives the weather. Energy from the sun, known as **solar radiation**, warms Earth. In some places it may be very hot or very cold, but it is always just right to support life. This is due to the **greenhouse effect**.

Like the glass in a greenhouse, gases in the atmosphere prevent too much heat from escaping from Earth's surface back into space. This natural greenhouse effect makes life on Earth possible.

The Greenhouse Effect

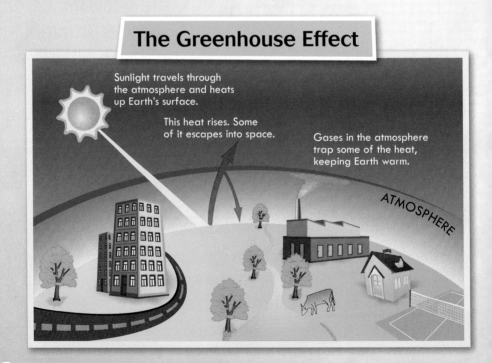

Sunlight travels through the atmosphere and heats up Earth's surface.

This heat rises. Some of it escapes into space.

Gases in the atmosphere trap some of the heat, keeping Earth warm.

ATMOSPHERE

The sun doesn't warm Earth equally. So hot places don't keep getting hotter and cold places colder; Earth keeps a balance. It does this by transferring heat from the equator, where it is hottest, to the poles, where it is coldest.

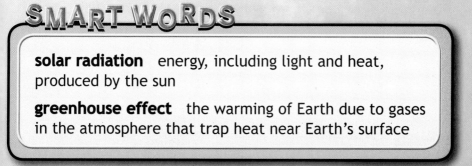

North Pole

Cold air

Equator

Warm air

Cold air

South Pole

Warm air near the equator rises and moves toward the poles. Cold air near the poles sinks and moves toward the equator. This constant flow of air between the equator and the poles creates patterns of air movement around Earth that affect the weather.

SMART WORDS

solar radiation   energy, including light and heat, produced by the sun

greenhouse effect   the warming of Earth due to gases in the atmosphere that trap heat near Earth's surface

What Causes Different Climates?

If Earth were flat, solar radiation would be the same everywhere. It would be like shining a light on a flat wall. But Earth is round. Solar radiation travels in straight-line paths called rays. The sun's rays do not strike all parts of Earth in the same way.

The sun's rays hit Earth most directly at the equator. As a result, the climate is hot and warm all year long in places along the equator.

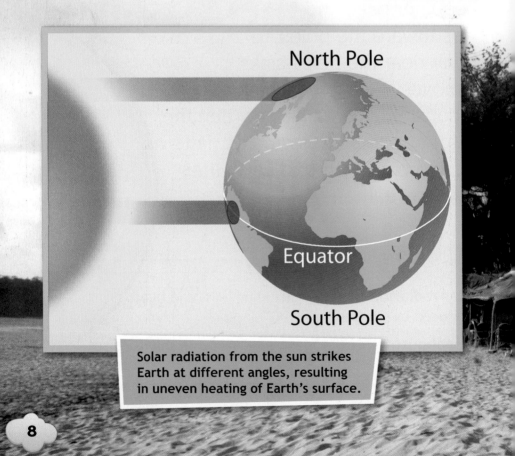

Solar radiation from the sun strikes Earth at different angles, resulting in uneven heating of Earth's surface.

North and south of the equator, the sun's rays hit at a slant, or angle. The result is that Earth's surface in those areas is not heated as much as where the sun's rays strike directly. Climates get gradually cooler as the distance from the equator increases.

The sun's rays strike Earth's surface at the greatest angle at the North and South Poles. As you might expect, the climate in those regions is colder than anywhere else on Earth.

Tropical areas around the equator are warm all year round. No heat is required in these houses!

The part of Earth tilted toward the sun experiences summer.

Reasons for the Seasons

You don't feel it, but Earth is in motion. Earth moves in a path called an **orbit** around the sun. It also spins like a top on an imaginary line called an **axis**. Earth's axis is slightly tilted. Because of the tilt, parts of Earth point toward or away from the sun as Earth moves through its orbit.

When the Northern Hemisphere points toward the sun, the sun's rays strike it more directly. This causes the longer days and warmer weather of summer.

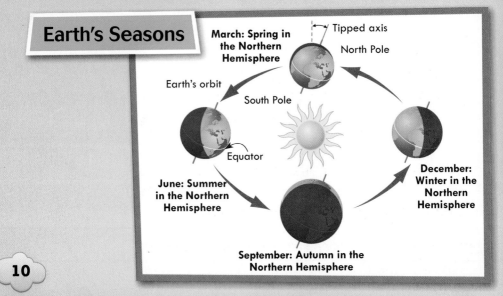

Earth's Seasons

March: Spring in the Northern Hemisphere

Tipped axis

North Pole

Earth's orbit

South Pole

Equator

June: Summer in the Northern Hemisphere

December: Winter in the Northern Hemisphere

September: Autumn in the Northern Hemisphere

The part of Earth tilted away from the sun experiences winter.

At the same time, the Southern Hemisphere is tilted away from the sun. It experiences the shorter days and cooler temperatures of winter.

When the Northern Hemisphere points away from the sun, it has winter. The Southern Hemisphere points toward the sun and has summer. During spring and autumn, neither hemisphere points toward or away from the sun.

The parts of the year marked by different weather and hours of daylight are known as the **seasons**.

SMART WORDS

orbit   the path of one object, such as Earth, as it moves around another object, such as the sun

axis   the imaginary line around which an object, such as Earth, rotates

season   one of four yearly patterns of weather that include spring, summer, autumn, and winter, that results from Earth's tilt and orbit

Use your SMART WORDS

Answer each question with a Smart Word.

atmosphere   weather   climate   orbit   axis
solar radiation   greenhouse effect   season

1. What term describes the long-term weather conditions in an area?
2. What is the path through which Earth travels around the sun?
3. What effect is responsible for keeping Earth warm enough to support life?
4. What is the blanket of air that surrounds Earth?
5. What name describes summer, winter, spring, or autumn?
6. What term describes the energy that travels from the sun to Earth?
7. What is the condition of the atmosphere in a specific place at any given time?
8. What is the imaginary line about which Earth rotates?

Answers on page 32

Talk Like a Scientist

Imagine that you have to teach a group of kindergartners. Use your Smart Words to explain the difference between weather and climate.

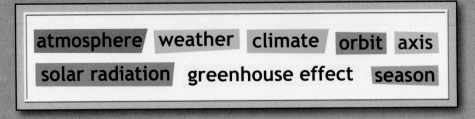

SMART FACTS

Did You Know?

The atmosphere is described by five different layers. Weather occurs in the troposphere, which is the layer closest to Earth's surface.

Good to Know

The second layer of the atmosphere, the stratosphere, contains ozone. This gas absorbs harmful radiation from the sun, protecting living things on Earth.

That's Amazing!

In a high layer known as the thermosphere, the air can get downright hot. That's because the air absorbs so much solar radiation from the sun.

EXOSPHERE

THERMOSPHERE

MESOSPHERE

STRATOSPHERE

TROPOSPHERE

Chapter 2

DESCRIBING THE

Weather

What would you say if someone asked you what the weather is like today? You would probably mention if it is hot or cold. Perhaps you would tell if it is rainy or sunny.

There are four main factors that interact to produce weather. They are:

- how hot or cold the air is
- how heavy the air is
- how much water is in the air
- how the air is moving

The weather forecast for these pups is sunny and clear. Perfect for a day at the beach!

| Sunny | Rainy | Cloudy | Partly sunny |

A map uses symbols to show weather conditions in different parts of the country.

Although each factor can be measured on its own, one always affects the others to produce different weather conditions. For example, how hot or cold an area is affects the weight of the air above it. This affects how the air will move.

All of this information might be presented on a weather map. A weather map is a picture that shows the kind of weather conditions occurring in different places.

The Hot and Cold of It

When you describe how hot or cold the air is, you are describing **temperature**. The tool you would use to measure temperature is a **thermometer**. Temperature is measured in units called degrees (°). Sometimes temperature is measured in units called degrees Fahrenheit (°F). Other times you might see metric units called degrees Celsius (°C). Low temperatures mean that it is cold outside. High temperatures mean it is hot.

Water freezes at a temperature of 32°F (0°C). That makes plenty of ice for these penguins to play on.

When the humidity is high — close to 100 percent — the water vapor in the air close to the ground can change from a gas to a liquid. The tiny liquid drops of water create fog.

Water in the Air

You can't see it, but there is water all around you. Air contains water vapor, which is water in the gas state. The amount of water vapor in the air is called **humidity**.

Most of the water vapor in the air comes from water that has evaporated, or changed from a liquid to a gas. Air that is over oceans or lakes usually has a large amount of water vapor, or high humidity. Air over drier land, such as deserts, has less water vapor, or low humidity.

SMART WORDS

temperature   a measure of how hot or cold something is

thermometer   a tool used to measure the temperature of a substance

humidity   the amount of water vapor in the air

The Weight of Air

As the air pressure changes, the needle on the barometer moves. It points to a number telling you what the air pressure is.

Air pressure is a measure of the weight of the air pressing down on an area. You can measure air pressure with a tool called a **barometer**. In an area of high pressure, the air particles are packed close together. The air particles are spread apart in an area of low pressure.

As you have read, cold air has more particles than warm air in the same amount of space. Places that are cool usually have higher air pressure than places that are warm.

SMART WORDS

air pressure   the weight of the air at any particular point on Earth

barometer   a tool used to measure air pressure

wind   the flow of air from a region of high pressure to a region of low pressure

anemometer   a tool used to measure wind speed

Winds Are Blowing

Air always moves from a region of high pressure to a region of low pressure as **wind**. You can determine the direction of wind with a weather vane. You can measure the speed of wind with a tool called an **anemometer**.

You may see winds on a weather map described by a direction and a speed. The direction tells you the direction from which the wind is blowing.

A weather vane tells you the direction of wind. A westerly wind blows from west to east.

W   E

Read each clue. Choose the Smart Word it describes.

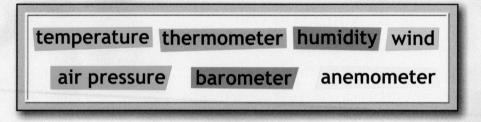

temperature thermometer humidity wind

air pressure barometer anemometer

1. I am a tool used to measure wind speed.

2. I am the weight of the air at any particular point on Earth.

3. I am a tool used to measure air pressure.

4. I am a measure of how hot or cold air is.

5. I am a tool that is used to measure the temperature of a substance.

6. I am water vapor in the air.

7. I am the flow of air from a region of high pressure to a region of low pressure.

Answers on page 32

Talk Like a Scientist

Pretend that you are going to give a weather report. Name and describe conditions of the atmosphere that you would include in your description. Be sure to use your Smart Words.

SMART FACTS

Record Breaker

The coldest place on Earth is in Antarctica, near the South Pole, where temperatures were recorded at more than 128°F (89°C) below zero!

That's Amazing!

Tropical rain forests have some of the highest humidity in the world. The air almost always holds about 80 percent of the possible water vapor it can.

Record Breaker

One of the hottest places on Earth is Death Valley in California. Temperatures have been recorded higher than 130°F (54°C).

Chapter 3

Rain or Shine?

Putting all the factors that affect weather together to predict weather conditions is no easy task. Scientists who study the weather are called **meteorologists**. They use data gathered from many tools and locations to create a **forecast**, which is a description of what they think weather conditions will be like in the near future.

A weather balloon is one of the earliest technologies used to gather information about the atmosphere.

SMART WORDS

meteorologist a scientist who works to understand, explain, and predict weather

forecast a prediction of weather conditions in the near future

precipitation any form of water, including rain, snow, and sleet, that falls from the clouds to Earth's surface

Accurate weather forecasts depend on information from weather stations located all around the world.

Some weather data comes from weather stations. A weather station has different kinds of instruments to measure temperature, air pressure, humidity, and wind. The instruments might also measure **precipitation**, which is water that falls from the atmosphere to Earth's surface. Rain, snow, and sleet are types of precipitation.

Other data comes from weather balloons, which carry instruments into the atmosphere. Some data even comes from weather satellites orbiting in space.

Weather satellites orbit Earth, collecting information about the atmosphere from all over the world.

Weather Patterns

The atmosphere contains large sections of air, called air masses. A **front** forms where two different air masses meet. Fronts form along the boundaries between warm air masses and cold air masses.

- A cold front forms when a cold air mass replaces a warm air mass. The temperature can drop dramatically when a cold front passes through.

- A warm front forms when a warm air mass replaces a cooler air mass. The air becomes warmer and more humid.

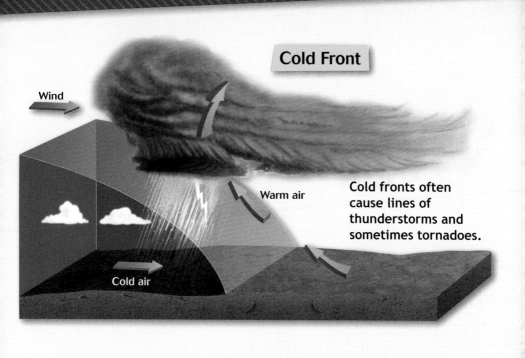

Cold Front

Wind

Warm air

Cold air

Cold fronts often cause lines of thunderstorms and sometimes tornadoes.

Warm Front

Warm air

Cold air

Warm fronts often bring light rain and fog.

SMART WORD

front   a region where two air masses of different temperatures meet

Controlling the Weather

Precipitation is necessary for growing crops and filling waterways. Too much precipitation, however, can lead to floods. Too little precipitation can lead to a **drought**. Both flooding and droughts can cause tremendous damage to land and food supplies.

Imagine if scientists could control the amount of rain that falls. Guess what? They can! Scientists have developed a method of controlling rainfall called cloud seeding.

These rockets will shoot from the ground to the clouds, where they will release silver iodide crystals.

SMART WORD

drought a period in which less precipitation than normal falls

As an airplane flies through the sky, it releases silver iodide crystals from the canisters attached to it.

Cloud seeding involves spreading materials into clouds to help them form precipitation. The materials might be dry ice or crystals of a chemical called silver iodide. The materials cause ice crystals to form in the top parts of clouds that become heavy enough to fall as snow, hail, or rain.

How do you get the materials into the clouds? Some methods involve using airplanes that drop them into clouds. Others use small rockets or other devices to shoot the materials from the ground into the clouds.

Match each description with the correct Smart Word.

meteorologist   precipitation

forecast   front   drought

1. any kind of water that falls from clouds to Earth's surface

2. a period in which less precipitation than normal falls

3. a prediction of what weather conditions might occur in the near future

4. a scientist who studies weather

5. a region where two air masses of different temperatures meet

Answers on page 32

Talk Like a Scientist

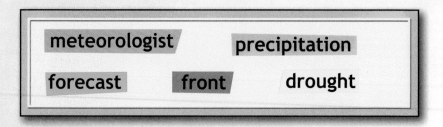

Explain the difference between the two kinds of fronts. Use Smart Words in your explanation.

SMART FACTS

How Interesting

Thin, wispy clouds that sometimes look like feathers are cirrus clouds. Found high up in the atmosphere, they occur in fair weather and are made up of ice crystals.

Did You Know?

The tallest of all the clouds are known as cumulonimbus clouds. They can produce lightning, thunder, heavy rains, and strong winds.

That's Amazing!

Stratus clouds are usually the lowest clouds in the sky. They can look like a gray blanket across the sky. Fog is a stratus cloud on the ground.

air pressure the weight of the air at any particular point on Earth

anemometer a tool used to measure wind speed

atmosphere the blanket of air that surrounds Earth

axis the imaginary line around which an object, such as Earth, rotates

barometer a tool used to measure air pressure

climate the long-term weather conditions in a region

drought a period in which less precipitation than normal falls

forecast a prediction of weather conditions in the near future

front a region where two air masses of different temperatures meet

greenhouse effect the warming of Earth due to gases in the atmosphere that trap heat near Earth's surface

humidity   the amount of water vapor in the air

meteorologist   a scientist who works to understand, explain, and predict weather

orbit   the path of one object, such as Earth, as it moves around another object, such as the sun

precipitation   any form of water, including rain, snow, and sleet, that falls from clouds to Earth's surface

season   one of four yearly patterns of weather that include spring, summer, autumn, and winter, that results from Earth's tilt and orbit

solar radiation   energy, including light and heat, produced by the sun

temperature   a measure of how hot or cold something is

thermometer   a tool used to measure the temperature of a substance

weather   the condition of the atmosphere at any given time in a particular location

wind   the flow of air from a region of high pressure to a region of low pressure

Index

SMART WORDS Answer Key

Page 12
1. climate, 2. orbit, 3. greenhouse effect, 4. atmosphere,
5. season, 6. solar radiation, 7. weather, 8. axis

Page 20
1. anemometer, 2. air pressure, 3. barometer, 4. temperature,
5. thermometer, 6. humidity, 7. wind

Page 28
1. precipitation, 2. drought, 3. forecast, 4. meteorologist, 5. front